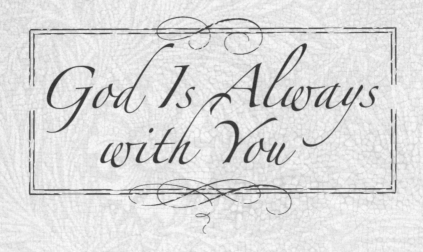

God Is Always with You

Promise Journal

God Is Always with You

Compiled by Joanie Garborg
Designed by Mick Thurber

Scripture references are from the following sources: The Holy Bible, King James Version (KJV). The Holy Bible, New International Version® NIV®. Copyright © 1973, 1978, 1984 International Bible Society. Used by permission of Zondervan Bible Publishers. The New American Standard Bible® (NASB), Copyright © 1960, 1962, 1963, 1968, 1971, 1972, 1973, 1975, 1977, 1995 by The Lockman Foundation. Used by permission. The Holy Bible, New Living Translation (NLT), copyright 1996. Used by permission of Tyndale House Publishers, Inc., Wheaton, Illinois 60189. All rights reserved. The Message, Copyright © 1993, 1994, 1995, 1996, 2000. 2001, 2002 by Eugene Peterson. Used by permission of NavPress, Colorado Springs, CO. The New Revised Standard Version Bible: Anglicized Edition (NRSV), copyright 1989, 1995, Division of Christian Education of the National Council of the Churches of Christ in the United States of America. All rights reserved. The Living Bible (TLB) © 1971. Used by permission of Tyndale House Publishers, Inc., Wheaton, Illinois 60189. All rights reserved.

Excluding Scripture verses, references to men and masculine pronouns have been replaced with gender-neutral references.

ISBN-13: 978-1-935416-98-2

Printed in China

To

_____

From

_____

LAKE HOUSE
GIFTS

EVER PRESENT

When I walk by the wayside, He is along with me.... Amid all my forgetfulness of Him, He never forgets me.

THOMAS CHALMERS

There's not a tint that paints the rose

Or decks the lily fair,

Or marks the humblest flower that grows,

But God has placed it there....

There's not a place on earth's vast round,

In ocean's deep or air,

Where love and beauty are not found,

For God is everywhere.

At every moment, God is calling your name and waiting to be found. To each cry of "Oh Lord," God answers, "I am here."

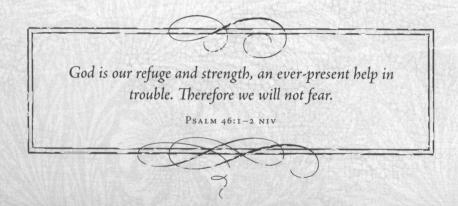

God is our refuge and strength, an ever-present help in trouble. Therefore we will not fear.

PSALM 46:1–2 NIV

EVER PRESENT

SHEPHERD AND GUARDIAN

He shall feed his flock like a shepherd: he shall gather the lambs with his arm, and carry them in his bosom, and shall gently lead those that are with young.

ISAIAH 40:11 KJV

All we like sheep have gone astray; we have turned every one to his own way; and the Lord hath laid on him the iniquity of us all.

ISAIAH 53:6 KJV

You were continually straying like sheep, but now you have returned to the Shepherd and Guardian of your souls.

I PETER 2:25 NASB

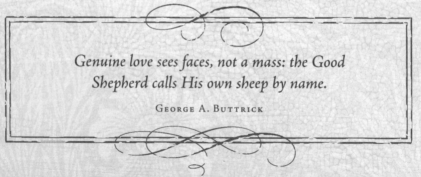

Genuine love sees faces, not a mass: the Good Shepherd calls His own sheep by name.

GEORGE A. BUTTRICK

SHEPHERD AND GUARDIAN

_____
_____
_____
_____
_____
_____
_____
_____
_____
_____
_____
_____
_____
_____
_____
_____
_____
_____
_____
_____
_____

COUNTLESS BEAUTIES

May God give you eyes to see beauty only the heart can understand.

From the world we see, hear, and touch, we behold inspired visions that reveal God's glory. In the sun's light, we catch warm rays of grace and glimpse His eternal design. In the birds' song, we hear His voice and it reawakens our desire for Him. At the wind's touch, we feel His Spirit and sense our eternal existence.

All the world is an utterance of the Almighty. Its countless beauties, its exquisite adaptations, all speak to you of Him.

PHILLIPS BROOKS

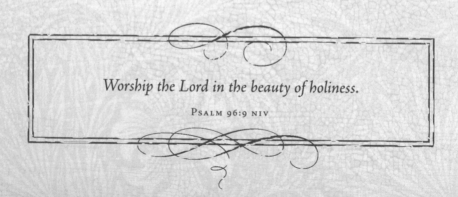

Worship the Lord in the beauty of holiness.

PSALM 96:9 NIV

COUNTLESS BEAUTIES

THE GRACE OF GOD

But God, being rich in mercy, because of His great love with which He loved us, even when we were dead in our transgressions, made us alive together with Christ (by grace you have been saved), and raised us up with Him, and seated us with Him in the heavenly places in Christ Jesus, so that in the ages to come He might show the surpassing riches of His grace in kindness toward us in Christ Jesus. For by grace you have been saved through faith; and that not of yourselves, it is the gift of God; not as a result of works, so that no one may boast. For we are His workmanship, created in Christ Jesus for good works, which God prepared beforehand so that we would walk in them.

EPHESIANS 2:4–10 NASB

Grace means that God already loves us as much as an infinite God can possibly love.

PHILIP YANCEY

THE GRACE OF GOD

E X P E C T A N T   R E V E R E N C E

God is within all things, but not included; outside all things, but not excluded, above all things, but not beyond their reach.

POPE ST. GREGORY I

There is a unique kind of transparence about things and events. The world is seen through, and no veil can conceal God completely. So those who are pious are ever alert to see behind the appearance of things a trace of the divine, and thus their attitude toward life is one of expectant reverence.

ABRAHAM JOSHUA HESCHEL

Because God created the Natural—invented it out of His love and artistry— it demands our reverence.

C. S. LEWIS

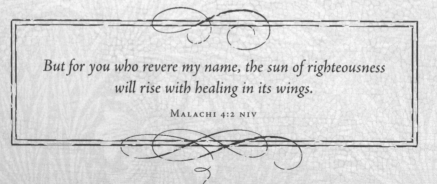

But for you who revere my name, the sun of righteousness will rise with healing in its wings.

MALACHI 4:2 NIV

EXPECTANT REVERENCE

OUR GRACIOUS GOD

Yet the Lord longs to be gracious to you; he rises to show you compassion. For the Lord is a God of justice. Blessed are all who wait for him!

ISAIAH 30:18 NIV

He made known his ways to Moses, his deeds to the people of Israel: The Lord is compassionate and gracious, slow to anger, abounding in love.

PSALM 103:7–8 NIV

O Lord, be gracious to us; we long for you. Be our strength every morning, our salvation in time of distress.

ISAIAH 33:2 NIV

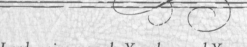

Lord…give me only Your love and Your grace. With this I am rich enough, and I have no more to ask.

IGNATIUS OF LOYOLA

OUR GRACIOUS GOD

THE GOODNESS OF GOD

The goodness of God is infinitely more wonderful than we will ever be able to comprehend.

A. W. TOZER

All that is good, all that is true, all that is beautiful, all that is beneficent, be it great or small, be it perfect or fragmentary, natural as well as supernatural, moral as well as material, comes from God.

CARDINAL JOHN HENRY NEWMAN

We walk without fear, full of hope and courage and strength to do His will, waiting for the endless good which He is always giving as fast as He can get us able to take it in.

GEORGE MACDONALD

Open your mouth and taste, open your eyes and see—how good God is. Blessed are you who run to him. Worship God if you want the best; worship opens doors to all his goodness.

PSALM 34:8–9 MSG

THE GOODNESS OF GOD

THE MAJESTY OF GOD

O Lord, our Lord, how majestic is your name in all the earth! You have set your glory above the heavens. When I consider your heavens, the work of your fingers, the moon and the stars, which you have set in place, what is man that you are mindful of him, the son of man that you care for him? You made him a little lower than the heavenly beings and crowned him with glory and honor. O Lord, our Lord, how majestic is your name in all the earth!

PSALM 8:1–5, 9 NIV

Savor little glimpses of God's goodness and His majesty,
thankful for the gift of them.

THE MAJESTY OF GOD

GOD DRAWS NEAR

When you are lonely I wish you love;

When you are down I wish you joy;

When you are troubled I wish you peace;

When things are complicated I wish you simple beauty;

When things are chaotic I wish you inner silence;

When things seem empty I wish you hope,

And the sweet sense of God's presence every passing day.

God still draws near to us in the ordinary, commonplace, everyday experiences and places.... He comes in surprising ways.

HENRY GARIEPY

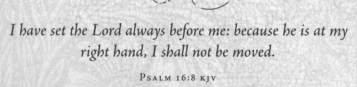

I have set the Lord always before me: because he is at my right hand, I shall not be moved.

PSALM 16:8 KJV

GOD DRAWS NEAR

THE POWER OF GOD

Search high and low, scan skies and land, you'll find nothing and no one quite like God. The holy angels are in awe before him; he looms immense and august over everyone around him. God of the Angel Armies, who is like you, powerful and faithful from every angle?

PSALM 89:6–8 MSG

Yours, O Lord, is the greatness and the power and the glory and the majesty and the splendor, for everything in heaven and earth is yours. Yours, O Lord, is the kingdom; you are exalted as head over all.

1 CHRONICLES 29:11 NIV

Ah, Sovereign Lord, you have made the heavens and the earth by your great power and outstretched arm. Nothing is too hard for you.

JEREMIAH 32:17 NIV

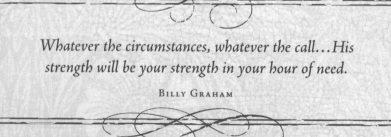

Whatever the circumstances, whatever the call…His strength will be your strength in your hour of need.

BILLY GRAHAM

THE POWER OF GOD

_____

_____

_____

_____

_____

_____

_____

_____

_____

_____

_____

_____

_____

_____

_____

_____

_____

_____

MADE FOR JOY

Our hearts were made for joy. Our hearts were made to enjoy the One who created them. Too deeply planted to be much affected by the ups and downs of life, this joy is a knowing and a being known by our Creator. He sets our hearts alight with radiant joy.

If one is joyful, it means that one is faithfully living for God, and that nothing else counts; and if one gives joy to others one is doing God's work. With joy without and joy within, all is well.

JANET ERSKINE STUART

Live for today but hold your hands open to tomorrow. Anticipate the future and its changes with joy. There is a seed of God's love in every event, every circumstance, every unpleasant situation in which you may find yourself.

BARBARA JOHNSON

The joy of the Lord is your strength.

NEHEMIAH 8:10 KJV

MADE FOR JOY

_____

_____

_____

_____

_____

_____

_____

_____

_____

_____

_____

_____

_____

_____

_____

_____

_____

_____

LOVE LIKE THAT

Watch what God does, and then you do it, like children who learn proper behavior from their parents. Mostly what God does is love you. Keep company with him and learn a life of love. Observe how Christ loved us. His love was not cautious but extravagant. He didn't love in order to get something from us but to give everything of himself to us. Love like that.

EPHESIANS 5:1–2 MSG

I pray that your love for each other will overflow more and more, and that you will keep on growing in your knowledge and understanding.

PHILIPPIANS 1:9 NLT

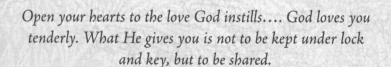

*Open your hearts to the love God instills…. God loves you
tenderly. What He gives you is not to be kept under lock
and key, but to be shared.*

MOTHER TERESA

LOVE LIKE THAT

FAITH ADVENTURE

There will always be the unknown. There will always be the unprovable. But faith confronts those frontiers with a thrilling leap. Then life becomes vibrant with adventure!

ROBERT SCHULLER

Faith means you want God and want to want nothing else.... In faith there is movement and development. Each day something is new.

BRENNAN MANNING

Faith sees the invisible, believes the incredible, and receives the impossible.

Faith is not a sense, not sight, not reason, but a taking God at His Word.

EVANS

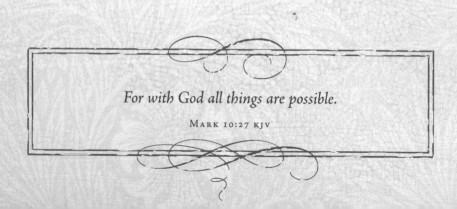

For with God all things are possible.

MARK 10:27 KJV

FAITH ADVENTURE

THE GREAT COMMISSION

Go therefore and make disciples of all the nations, baptizing them in the name of the Father and the Son and the Holy Spirit, teaching them to observe all that I commanded you; and lo, I am with you always, even to the end of the age.

MATTHEW 28:19–20 NASB

But do not let this one fact escape your notice, beloved, that with the Lord one day is like a thousand years, and a thousand years like one day. The Lord is not slow about His promise, as some count slowness, but is patient toward you, not wishing for any to perish but for all to come to repentance.

2 PETER 3:8–9 NASB

My purpose is that…they may have the full riches of complete understanding, in order that they may know the mystery of God, namely, Christ, in whom are hidden all the treasures of wisdom and knowledge.

COLOSSIANS 2:2–3 NIV

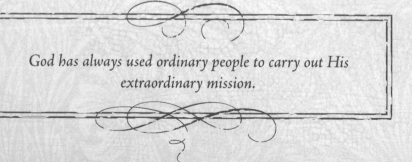

God has always used ordinary people to carry out His extraordinary mission.

THE GREAT COMMISSION

A LIFE TRANSFORMED

To pray is to change. This is a great grace. How good of God to provide a path whereby our lives can be taken over by love and joy and peace and patience and kindness and goodness and faithfulness and gentleness and self-control.

RICHARD J. FOSTER

For God is, indeed, a wonderful Father who longs to pour out His mercy upon us, and whose majesty is so great that He can transform us from deep within.

TERESA OF AVILA

A life transformed by the power of God is always a marvel and a miracle.

GERALDINE NICHOLAS

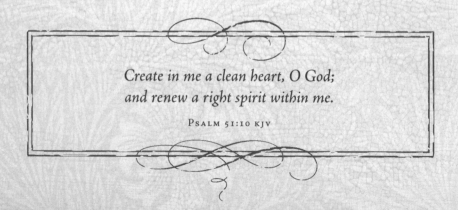

*Create in me a clean heart, O God;
and renew a right spirit within me.*

PSALM 51:10 KJV

A LIFE TRANSFORMED

_____

_____

_____

_____

_____

_____

_____

_____

_____

_____

_____

_____

_____

_____

_____

_____

_____

_____

_____

GOD'S CARE

The Lord is my shepherd; I shall not want. He maketh me to lie down in green pastures: he leadeth me beside the still waters. He restoreth my soul: he leadeth me in the paths of righteousness for his name's sake. Yea, though I walk through the valley of the shadow of death, I will fear no evil: for thou art with me; thy rod and thy staff they comfort me. Thou preparest a table before me in the presence of mine enemies: thou anointest my head with oil; my cup runneth over. Surely goodness and mercy shall follow me all the days of my life: and I will dwell in the house of the Lord for ever.

PSALM 23:1–6 KJV

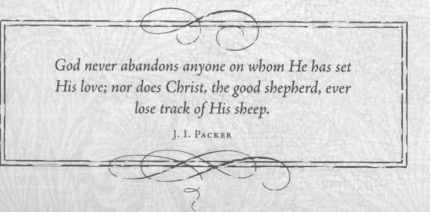

God never abandons anyone on whom He has set His love; nor does Christ, the good shepherd, ever lose track of His sheep.

J. I. PACKER

GOD'S CARE

THE ROAD AHEAD

My Lord God, I have no idea where I am going. I do not see the road ahead of me. I cannot know for certain where it will end.... But I believe that the desire to please You does in fact please You. And I hope I have that desire in all that I am doing. I hope that I will never do anything apart from that desire. And I know that if I do this, You will lead me by the right road though I may know nothing about it. Therefore will I trust You always though I may seem to be lost and in the shadow of death. I will not fear, for You are ever with me. And You will never leave me to face my perils alone.

THOMAS MERTON

I would rather walk with God in the dark than go alone in the light.

MARY GARDINER BRAINARD

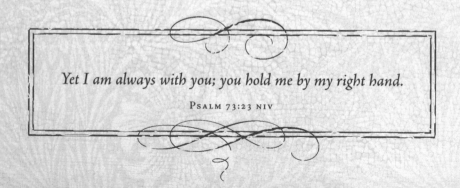

Yet I am always with you; you hold me by my right hand.

PSALM 73:23 NIV

THE ROAD AHEAD

RENEWING WORD

You're my place of quiet retreat; I wait for your Word to renew me…. Therefore I lovingly embrace everything you say.

PSALM 119:114, 119 MSG

You have dealt well with Your servant, O Lord, according to Your word. Teach me good discernment and knowledge, for I believe in Your commandments. Before I was afflicted I went astray, but now I keep Your word. You are good and do good; teach me Your statutes.

PSALM 119:65–68 NASB

All your words are true; all your righteous laws are eternal.

PSALM 119:160

Be still, and in the quiet moments, listen to the voice of your heavenly Father. His words can renew your spirit…no one knows you and your needs like He does.

JANET L. WEAVER SMITH

RENEWING WORD

GRACE REVEALED

Look deep within yourself and recognize what brings life and grace into your heart. It is this that can be shared with those around you. You are loved by God. This is an inspiration to love.

CHRISTOPHER DE VINCK

All God's glory and beauty come from within, and there He delights to dwell. His visits there are frequent, His conversation sweet, His comforts refreshing, His peace passing all understanding.

THOMAS À KEMPIS

The Lord's chief desire is to reveal Himself to you and, in order for Him to do that, He gives you abundant grace. The Lord gives you the experience of enjoying His presence. He touches you, and His touch is so delightful that, more than ever, you are drawn inwardly to Him.

MADAME JEANNE GUYON

Set your hope fully on the grace to be given you when Jesus Christ is revealed.

1 PETER 1:13 NIV

GRACE REVEALED

_____

_____

_____

_____

_____

_____

_____

_____

_____

_____

_____

_____

_____

_____

_____

_____

_____

_____

_____

_____

_____

_____

RESTORATION

The Spirit of the Sovereign Lord is on me, because the Lord has anointed me to preach good news to the poor. He has sent me to bind up the brokenhearted, to proclaim freedom for the captives and release from darkness for the prisoners, to proclaim the year of the Lord's favor and the day of vengeance of our God, to comfort all who mourn, and provide for those who grieve in Zion—to bestow on them a crown of beauty instead of ashes, the oil of gladness instead of mourning, and a garment of praise instead of a spirit of despair. They will be called oaks of righteousness, a planting of the Lord for the display of his splendor.

ISAIAH 61:1–3 NIV

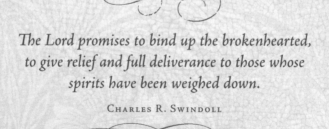

The Lord promises to bind up the brokenhearted,
to give relief and full deliverance to those whose
spirits have been weighed down.

CHARLES R. SWINDOLL

RESTORATION

For Himself

Although it be good to think upon the kindness of God, and to love Him and worship Him for it; yet it is far better to gaze upon the pure essence of Him and to love Him and worship Him for himself.

We desire many things, and God offers us only one thing. He can offer us only one thing—himself. He has nothing else to give. There is nothing else to give.

<small>Peter Kreeft</small>

The reason for loving God is God himself, and the measure in which we should love Him is to love Him without measure.

<small>Bernard of Clairvaux</small>

The Lord alone shall be exalted.

<small>Isaiah 2:11 KJV</small>

FOR HIMSELF

_____

_____

_____

_____

_____

_____

_____

_____

_____

_____

_____

_____

_____

_____

_____

_____

_____

_____

_____

_____

GOD'S THOUGHTS

Your thoughts—how rare, how beautiful! God, I'll never comprehend them! I couldn't even begin to count them—any more than I could count the sand of the sea. Oh, let me rise in the morning and live always with you!

PSALM 139:17–18 MSG

The counsel of the Lord standeth for ever, the thoughts of his heart to all generations.

PSALM 33:11 KJV

How great are your works, O Lord, how profound your thoughts!

PSALM 92:5 NIV

"My thoughts are completely different from yours," says the Lord. "And my ways are far beyond anything you could imagine. For just as the heavens are higher than the earth, so are my ways higher than your ways and my thoughts higher than your thoughts."

ISAIAH 55:8–9 NLT

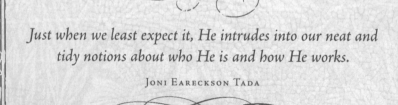

Just when we least expect it, He intrudes into our neat and tidy notions about who He is and how He works.

JONI EARECKSON TADA

GOD'S THOUGHTS

_____

_____

_____

_____

_____

_____

_____

_____

_____

_____

_____

_____

_____

_____

_____

_____

_____

_____

_____

_____

_____

His Presence

And I have felt

A presence that disturbs me with the joy

Of elevated thoughts; a sense sublime

Of something far more deeply interfused,

Whose dwelling is the light of setting suns.

WILLIAM WORDSWORTH

Know by the light of faith that God is present, and be content with directing all your

actions toward Him.

BROTHER LAWRENCE

God wants us to be present where we are. He invites us to see and to hear what is

around us and, through it all, to discern the footprints of the Holy.

RICHARD J. FOSTER

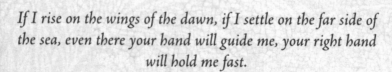

*If I rise on the wings of the dawn, if I settle on the far side of
the sea, even there your hand will guide me, your right hand
will hold me fast.*

PSALM 139:9–10 NIV

HIS PRESENCE

_____
_____
_____
_____
_____
_____
_____
_____
_____
_____
_____
_____
_____
_____
_____
_____
_____
_____
_____
_____
_____
_____
_____
_____

SEEK FIRST

Look at the birds of the air, that they do not sow, nor reap nor gather into barns, and yet your heavenly Father feeds them. Are you not worth much more than they? And who of you by being worried can add a single hour to his life? And why are you worried about clothing? Observe how the lilies of the field grow; they do not toil nor do they spin, yet I say to you that not even Solomon in all his glory clothed himself like one of these. But if God so clothes the grass of the field, which is alive today and tomorrow is thrown into the furnace, will He not much more clothe you? You of little faith! Do not worry then, saying, "What will we eat?" or "What will we drink?" or "What will we wear for clothing?" For…your heavenly Father knows that you need all these things. But seek first His kingdom and His righteousness, and all these things will be added to you.

MATTHEW 6:26–33 NASB

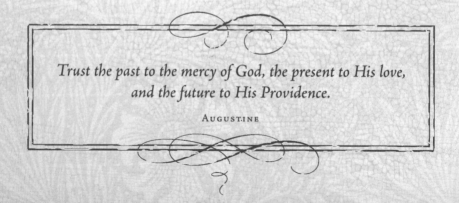

Trust the past to the mercy of God, the present to His love,
and the future to His Providence.

AUGUSTINE

SEEK FIRST

_____

_____

_____

_____

_____

_____

_____

_____

_____

_____

_____

_____

_____

_____

_____

_____

_____

_____

GOD WITH US

God gets down on His knees among us; gets on our level and shares Himself with us. He does not reside afar off and send diplomatic messages, He kneels among us…. God shares himself generously and graciously.

EUGENE PETERSON

You are in the Beloved…therefore infinitely dear to the Father, unspeakably precious to Him. You are never, not for one second, alone.

NORMAN DOWTY

We are never more fulfilled than when our longing for God is met by His presence in our lives.

BILLY GRAHAM

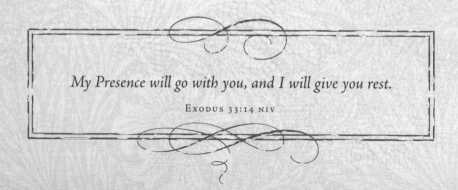

My Presence will go with you, and I will give you rest.

EXODUS 33:14 NIV

GOD WITH US

GOD'S PROMISES

Not one word of all the good words which the Lord your God spoke concerning you has failed; all have been fulfilled for you, not one of them has failed.

JOSHUA 23:14 NASB

The fulfillment of God's promise depends entirely on trusting God and his way, and then simply embracing him and what he does. God's promise arrives as pure gift.

ROMANS 4:16 MSG

Your promises have been thoroughly tested; that is why I love them so much.

PSALM 119:140 NLT

We may…depend upon God's promises, for…
He will be as good as His word.

MATTHEW HENRY

GOD'S PROMISES

NOTHING BUT GRACE

There is nothing but God's grace. We walk upon it; we breathe it; we live and die by it; it makes the nails and axles of the universe.

ROBERT LOUIS STEVENSON

Grace is no stationary thing, it is ever becoming. It is flowing straight out of God's heart. Grace does nothing but re-form and convey God. Grace makes the soul conformable to the will of God. God, the ground of the soul, and grace go together.

MEISTER ECKHART

Grace and gratitude belong together like heaven and earth. Grace evokes gratitude like the voice an echo. Gratitude follows grace as thunder follows lightning.

KARL BARTH

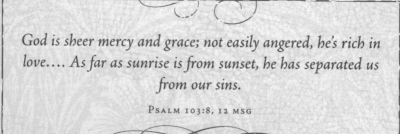

God is sheer mercy and grace; not easily angered, he's rich in love.... As far as sunrise is from sunset, he has separated us from our sins.

PSALM 103:8, 12 MSG

NOTHING BUT GRACE

THE STRONGHOLD

The Lord is my light and my salvation—whom shall I fear? The Lord is the stronghold of my life—of whom shall I be afraid? One thing I ask of the Lord, this is what I seek: that I may dwell in the house of the Lord all the days of my life, to gaze upon the beauty of the Lord and to seek him in his temple. For in the day of trouble he will keep me safe in his dwelling; he will hide me in the shelter of his tabernacle and set me high upon a rock. Hear my voice when I call, O Lord; be merciful to me and answer me. My heart says of you, "Seek his face!" Your face, Lord, I will seek.

PSALM 27:1, 4–5, 7–8 NIV

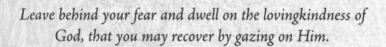

Leave behind your fear and dwell on the lovingkindness of God, that you may recover by gazing on Him.

THE STRONGHOLD

An Inner Place

Retire from the world each day to some private spot…. Stay in the secret place till the surrounding noises begin to fade out of your heart and a sense of God's presence envelops you…. Listen for the inward Voice till you learn to recognize it…. Give yourself to God and then be what and who you are without regard to what others think…. Learn to pray inwardly every moment.

A.W. TOZER

Within each of us there is an inner place where the living God himself longs to dwell, our sacred center of belief.

I will remember that when I give Him my heart, God chooses to live within me— body and soul. And I know He really is as close as breathing, His very Spirit inside of me.

*I pray that out of his glorious riches he may strengthen you
with power through his Spirit in your inner being.*

EPHESIANS 3:16 NIV

AN INNER PLACE

A PERSONAL GUIDE

But I'll take the hand of those who don't know the way, who can't see where they're going. I'll be a personal guide to them, directing them through unknown country. I'll be right there to show them what roads to take, make sure they don't fall into the ditch. These are the things I'll be doing for them—sticking with them, not leaving them for a minute.

ISAIAH 42:16 MSG

Whether you turn to the right or to the left, your ears will hear a voice behind you, saying, "This is the way; walk in it."

ISAIAH 30:21 NIV

We can make our plans, but the Lord determines our steps.

PROVERBS 16:9 NLT

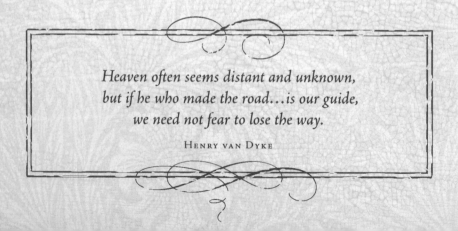

Heaven often seems distant and unknown,
but if he who made the road…is our guide,
we need not fear to lose the way.

HENRY VAN DYKE

A PERSONAL GUIDE

Treasure in Nature

If we are children of God, we have a tremendous treasure in nature and will realize that it is holy and sacred. We will see God reaching out to us in every wind that blows, every sunrise and sunset, every cloud in the sky, every flower that blooms, and every leaf that fades.

Oswald Chambers

The longer I live, the more my mind dwells upon the beauty and the wonder of the world.

John Burroughs

Look up at all the stars in the night sky and hear your Father saying, "I carefully set each one in its place. Know that I love you more than these." Sit by the lake's edge, listening to the water lapping the shore and hear your Father gently calling you to that place near His heart.

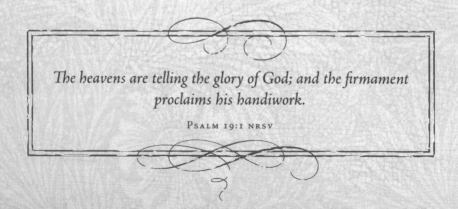

The heavens are telling the glory of God; and the firmament proclaims his handiwork.

Psalm 19:1 nrsv

TREASURE IN NATURE

DON'T BE AFRAID

Don't be afraid, I've redeemed you. I've called your name. You're mine. When you're in over your head, I'll be there with you. When you're in rough waters, you will not go down. When you're between a rock and a hard place, it won't be a dead end—Because I am God, your personal God, The Holy of Israel, your Savior. I paid a huge price for you…! *That's* how much you mean to me! *That's* how much I love you!

ISAIAH 43:1–4 MSG

If God be for us, who can be against us?

ROMANS 8:31 KJV

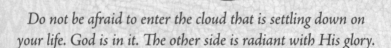

Do not be afraid to enter the cloud that is settling down on your life. God is in it. The other side is radiant with His glory.

L. B. COWMAN

DON'T BE AFRAID

Praise Him

When morning gilds the skies,
My heart awakening cries:
May Jesus Christ be praised!

Joseph Barnby

Does not all nature around me praise God? If I were silent, I should be an exception to the universe. Does not the thunder praise Him as it rolls like drums in the march of the God of armies? Do not the mountains praise Him when the woods upon their summits wave in adoration? Does not the lightning write His name in letters of fire? Has not the whole earth a voice? And shall I, can I, silent be?

C. H. Spurgeon

O God, great and wonderful, who has created the heavens, dwelling in the light and beauty of it...teach me to praise You, even as the lark which offers her song at daybreak.

Isidore of Seville

Then your light will break forth like the dawn, and your
healing will quickly appear; then your righteousness will go
before you, and the glory of the Lord will be your rear guard.

Isaiah 58:8 NIV

PRAISE HIM

_____

_____

_____

_____

_____

_____

_____

_____

_____

_____

_____

_____

_____

_____

_____

_____

_____

_____

_____

_____

_____

_____

HAVE MERCY

Search me, O God, and know my heart; test me and know my anxious thoughts. See if there is any offensive way in me, and lead me in the way everlasting.

PSALM 139:23–24 NIV

When my anxious thoughts multiply within me, your consolations delight my soul.

PSALM 94:19 NASB

Seek the Lord while he may be found, call upon him while he is near; let the wicked forsake their way, and the unrighteous their thoughts; let them return to the Lord, that he may have mercy on them, and to our God, for he will abundantly pardon.

ISAIAH 55:6–7 NRSV

We need more than a watchmaker who winds up the universe and lets it tick. We need love and mercy and forgiveness and grace—qualities only a personal God can offer.

PHILIP YANCEY

HAVE MERCY

_____

_____

_____

_____

_____

_____

_____

_____

_____

_____

_____

_____

_____

_____

_____

_____

_____

_____

_____

_____

_____

_____

Settled in Solitude

Solitude liberates us from entanglements by carving out a space from which we can see ourselves and our situation before the Audience of One. Solitude provides the private place where we can take our bearings and so make God our North Star.

Os Guinness

Settle yourself in solitude and you will come upon Him in yourself.

Teresa of Avila

We must drink deeply from the very Source the deep calm and peace of interior quietude and refreshment of God, allowing the pure water of divine grace to flow plentifully and unceasingly from the Source itself.

Mother Teresa

Whoever drinks of the water that I will give him shall never thirst; but the water that I will give him will become in him a well of water springing up to eternal life.

John 4:13–14 nasb

SETTLED IN SOLITUDE

_____

_____

_____

_____

_____

_____

_____

_____

_____

_____

_____

_____

_____

_____

_____

_____

_____

_____

_____

_____

_____

SHOWERS OF BLESSINGS

Bless the Lord, O my soul: and all that is within me, bless his holy name. Bless the Lord, O my soul, and forget not all his benefits: Who forgiveth all thine iniquities; who healeth all thy diseases; who redeemeth thy life from destruction; who crowneth thee with lovingkindness and tender mercies; who satisfieth thy mouth with good things; so that thy youth is renewed like the eagle's.

PSALM 103:1–5 KJV

I will send showers, showers of blessings, which will come just when they are needed.

EZEKIEL 34:26 NLT

The Lord bless you, and keep you; the Lord make His face shine on you, and be gracious to you; the Lord lift up His countenance on you, and give you peace.

NUMBERS 6:24–26 NIV

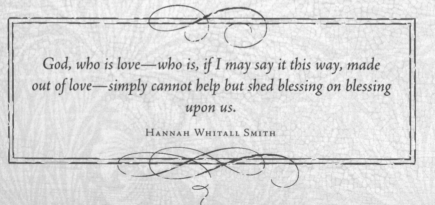

God, who is love—who is, if I may say it this way, made out of love—simply cannot help but shed blessing on blessing upon us.

HANNAH WHITALL SMITH

SHOWERS OF BLESSINGS

_____

_____

_____

_____

_____

_____

_____

_____

_____

_____

_____

_____

_____

_____

_____

_____

_____

_____

_____

FAITHFUL GUIDE

God, who has led you safely on so far, will lead you on to the end. Be altogether at rest in the loving holy confidence which you ought to have in His heavenly Providence.

FRANCIS DE SALES

Guidance is a sovereign act. Not merely does God will to guide us by showing us His way…whatever mistakes we may make, we shall come safely home. Slippings and strayings there will be, no doubt, but the everlasting arms are beneath us; we shall be caught, rescued, restored. This is God's promise; this is how good He is. And our self-distrust, while keeping us humble, must not cloud the joy with which we lean on our faithful covenant God.

J. I. PACKER

When we obey him, every path he guides us on is fragrant with his loving-kindness and his truth.

PSALM 25:10 TLB

FAITHFUL GUIDE

_____

_____

_____

_____

_____

_____

_____

_____

_____

_____

_____

_____

_____

_____

_____

_____

_____

_____

_____

_____

_____

GOD IS OUR REFUGE

Hear my cry, O God; Give heed to my prayer. From the end of the earth I call to You when my heart is faint; lead me to the rock that is higher than I. For You have been a refuge for me, a tower of strength against the enemy. Let me dwell in Your tent forever; let me take refuge in the shelter of Your wings.

PSALM 61:1–4 NASB

Whom have I in heaven but You? And besides You, I desire nothing on earth. My flesh and my heart may fail, but God is the strength of my heart and my portion forever. As for me, the nearness of God is my good; I have made the Lord God my refuge.

PSALM 73:25–26, 28 NASB

When God has become…our refuge and our fortress, then
we can reach out to Him in the midst of a broken world and
feel at home while still on the way.

HENRI J. M. NOUWEN

GOD IS OUR REFUGE

_____

_____

_____

_____

_____

_____

_____

_____

_____

_____

_____

_____

_____

_____

_____

_____

_____

_____

_____

ENCOUNTERING GOD

God is with us in the midst of our daily, routine lives. In the middle of cleaning the house or driving somewhere in the pickup.... Often it's in the middle of the most mundane task that He lets us know He is there with us. We realize, then, that there can be no "ordinary" moments for people who live their lives with Jesus.

MICHAEL CARD

Much of what is sacred is hidden in the ordinary, everyday moments of our lives. To see something of the sacred in those moments takes slowing down so we can live our lives more reflectively.

KEN GIRE

We encounter God in the ordinariness of life, not in the search for spiritual highs and extraordinary, mystical experiences, but in our simple presence in life.

BRENNAN MANNING

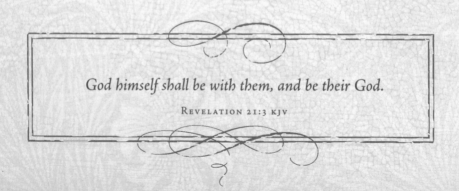

God himself shall be with them, and be their God.

REVELATION 21:3 KJV

ENCOUNTERING GOD

LOVE NEVER FAILS

If I speak with the tongues of men and of angels, but do not have love, I have become a noisy gong or a clanging cymbal. If I have the gift of prophecy, and know all mysteries and all knowledge; and if I have all faith, so as to remove mountains, but do not have love, I am nothing. And if I give all my possessions to feed the poor, and if I surrender my body to be burned, but do not have love, it profits me nothing. Love is patient, love is kind and is not jealous; love does not brag and is not arrogant, does not act unbecomingly; it does not seek its own, is not provoked, does not take into account a wrong suffered, does not rejoice in unrighteousness, but rejoices with the truth; bears all things, believes all things, hopes all things, endures all things. Love never fails.

1 CORINTHIANS 13:1–8 NASB

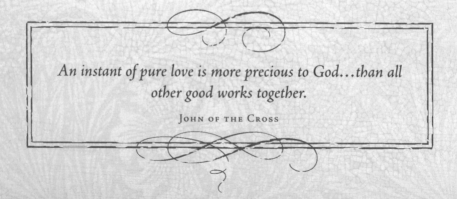

An instant of pure love is more precious to God…than all other good works together.

JOHN OF THE CROSS

LOVE NEVER FAILS

ENFOLDED IN PEACE

I will let God's peace infuse every part of today. As the chaos swirls and life's demands pull at me on all sides, I will breathe in God's peace that surpasses all understanding. He has promised that He would set within me a peace too deeply planted to be affected by unexpected or exhausting demands.

Calm me, O Lord, as you stilled the storm,
Still me, O Lord, keep me from harm.
Let all the tumult within me cease,
Enfold me, Lord, in your peace.

CELTIC TRADITIONAL

God cannot give us a happiness and peace apart from himself, because it is not there. There is no such thing.

C. S. LEWIS

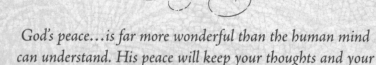

God's peace…is far more wonderful than the human mind can understand. His peace will keep your thoughts and your hearts quiet and at rest.

PHILIPPIANS 4:7 TLB

ENFOLDED IN PEACE

DOMINION

He raised [Christ] from the dead and seated him at his right hand in the heavenly realms, far above all rule and authority, power and dominion, and every title that can be given, not only in the present age but also in the one to come. And God placed all things under his feet and appointed him to be head over everything for the church, which is his body, the fullness of him who fills everything in every way.

EPHESIANS 1:20–22 NIV

Blessed be the name of God from age to age, for wisdom and power are his. He changes times and seasons, deposes kings and sets up kings; he gives wisdom to the wise and knowledge to those who have understanding. He reveals deep and hidden things; he knows what is in the darkness, and light dwells with him.

DANIEL 2:20–22 NRSV

For he is the living God and he endures forever; his kingdom will not be destroyed, his dominion will never end.

DANIEL 6:26 NIV

Today Jesus is working just as wonderful works as when He created the heaven and the earth. His wondrous grace, His wonderful omnipotence, is for His child who needs Him and who trusts Him, even today.

HURLBURT AND HORTON

DOMINION

SOUGHT AND FOUND

It is God's will that we believe that we see Him continually, though it seems to us that the sight be only partial; and through this belief He makes us always to gain more grace, for God wishes to be seen, and He wishes to be sought, and He wishes to be expected, and He wishes to be trusted.

JULIAN OF NORWICH

To seek God means first of all to let yourself be found by Him.

God's nature is given me. His love is jealous for my life. All His attributes are woven into the pattern of my spirit. What a God is this! His life implanted in every child. Thank you, Father, for this.

JIM ELLIOT

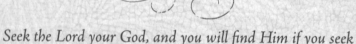

Seek the Lord your God, and you will find Him if you seek Him with all your heart and with all your soul.

DEUTERONOMY 4:29 NIV

SOUGHT AND FOUND

_____

_____

_____

_____

_____

_____

_____

_____

_____

_____

_____

_____

_____

_____

_____

_____

_____

_____

_____

_____

FREE TO LIVE

God, your God, will cut away the thick calluses on your heart and your children's hearts, freeing you to love God, your God, with your whole heart and soul and live, really live.... And you will make a new start, listening obediently to God, keeping all his commandments that I'm commanding you today. God, your God, will outdo himself in making things go well for you.... Love God, your God. Walk in his ways. Keep his commandments, regulations, and rules so that you will live, really live, live exuberantly, blessed by God.... Love God, your God, listening obediently to him, firmly embracing him. Oh yes, he is life itself.

DEUTERONOMY 30:6–9, 16, 20 MSG

*I asked God for all things that I might enjoy life. He gave
me life that I might enjoy all things.*

FREE TO LIVE

PRESS ON

Keep on going and chances are you will stumble on something, perhaps when you are least expecting it. I have never heard of anyone stumbling on something sitting down.

CHARLES F. KETTERING

When things go wrong, as they sometimes will,

When the road you're trudging seems all uphill,

When the funds are low and the debts are high,

And you want to smile, but you have to sigh,

When care is pressing you down a bit,

Rest, if you must—but don't you quit!

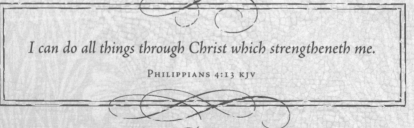

I can do all things through Christ which strengtheneth me.

PHILIPPIANS 4:13 KJV

PRESS ON

Water of Life

For I will pour water on the thirsty land, and streams on the dry ground; I will pour out my Spirit on your offspring, and my blessing on your descendants. They will spring up like grass in a meadow, like poplar trees by flowing streams.

Isaiah 44:3–4 NIV

The earth shall be filled with the knowledge of the glory of the Lord, as the waters cover the sea.

Habakkuk 2:14 KJV

Is anyone thirsty? Come!
All who will, come and drink,
Drink freely of the Water of Life!

Revelation 22:17 MSG

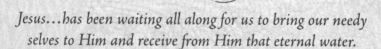

Jesus…has been waiting all along for us to bring our needy selves to Him and receive from Him that eternal water.

Doris Gailey

WATER OF LIFE

THE BEAUTY OF GOD'S PEACE

In comparison with this big world, the human heart is only a small thing. Though the world is so large, it is utterly unable to satisfy this tiny heart. Our ever growing soul and its capacities can be satisfied only in the infinite God. As water is restless until it reaches its level, so the soul has no peace until it rests in God.

SADHU SUNDAR SINGH

Peace is a margin of power around our daily need. Peace is a consciousness of springs too deep for earthly droughts to dry up.

HARRY EMERSON FOSDICK

Drop Thy still dews of quietness
till all our strivings cease;
take from our souls the strain and stress,
and let our ordered lives confess
the beauty of Thy peace.

JOHN GREENLEAF WHITTIER

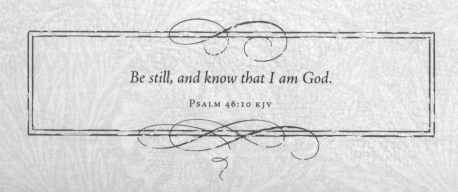

Be still, and know that I am God.

PSALM 46:10 KJV

THE BEAUTY OF GOD'S PEACE

_____

_____

_____

_____

_____

_____

_____

_____

_____

_____

_____

_____

_____

_____

_____

_____

_____

_____

_____

_____

_____

_____

_____

PERFECT PEACE

Be careful for nothing; but in every thing by prayer and supplication with thanksgiving let your requests be made known unto God. And the peace of God, which passeth all understanding, shall keep your hearts and minds through Christ Jesus.

PHILIPPIANS 4:6–7 KJV

You will keep in perfect peace him whose mind is steadfast, because he trusts in you. Trust in the Lord forever, for the Lord, the Lord, is the Rock eternal.

ISAIAH 26:3–4 NIV

Therefore being justified by faith, we have peace with God through our Lord Jesus Christ.

ROMANS 5:1 KJV

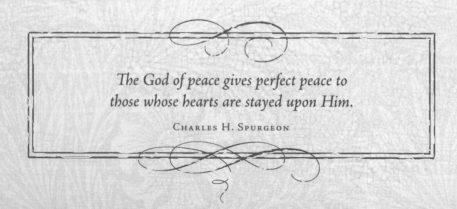

The God of peace gives perfect peace to those whose hearts are stayed upon Him.

CHARLES H. SPURGEON

PERFECT PEACE

_____

_____

_____

_____

_____

_____

_____

_____

_____

_____

_____

_____

_____

_____

_____

_____

_____

_____

_____

A FIRSTHAND EXPERIENCE

Listening to God is a firsthand experience…. God invites *you* to vacation in His splendor. He invites *you* to feel the touch of His hand. He invites *you* to feast at His table. He wants to spend time with *you*.

MAX LUCADO

Prayer is everywhere…. Prayer is language used to respond to the most that has been said to us, with the potential for saying all that is in us.

EUGENE PETERSON

In extravagance of soul we seek His face. In generosity of heart, we glean His gentle touch. In excessiveness of spirit, we love Him and His love comes back to us a hundredfold.

TRICIA McCARY RHODES

Trust steadily in God, hope unswervingly, love extravagantly. And the best of the three is love.

1 CORINTHIANS 13:13 MSG

A FIRSTHAND EXPERIENCE

_____

_____

_____

_____

_____

_____

_____

_____

_____

_____

_____

_____

_____

_____

_____

_____

_____

_____

_____

_____

GOD'S WORD

With my whole heart have I sought thee: O let me not wander from thy commandments. Thy word have I hid in mine heart, that I might not sin against thee.... I will not forget thy word.

PSALM 119:10–11, 16 KJV

All Scripture is God-breathed and is useful for teaching, rebuking, correcting and training in righteousness.

2 TIMOTHY 3:16 NIV

For the word of God is living and active and sharper than any two-edged sword, and piercing as far as the division of soul and spirit, of both joints and marrow, and able to judge the thoughts and intentions of the heart. And there is no creature hidden from His sight, but all things are open and laid bare to the eyes of Him with whom we have to do.

HEBREWS 4:12–13 NASB

When we give the Word of God space to live in our heart, the Spirit of God will use it to take root, penetrating the earthiest recesses of our lives.

KEN GIRE

GOD'S WORD

New Every Morning

Morning has broken like the first morning,

Blackbird has spoken like the first bird....

Praise with elation, praise every morning,

God's re-creation of the new day!

ELEANOR FARJEON

Always new. Always exciting. Always full of promise. The mornings of our lives, each

a personal daily miracle!

GLORIA GAITHER

That is God's call to us—simply to be people who are content to live close to Him

and to renew the kind of life in which the closeness is felt and experienced.

THOMAS MERTON

The steadfast love of the Lord never ceases,
his mercies never come to an end;
they are new every morning;
great is your faithfulness.

LAMENTATIONS 3:22–23 NRSV

NEW EVERY MORNING

THE LORD'S PRAYER

Our Father which art in heaven, Hallowed be thy name. Thy kingdom come. Thy will be done in earth, as it is in heaven. Give us this day our daily bread. And forgive us our debts, as we forgive our debtors. And lead us not into temptation, but deliver us from evil: For thine is the kingdom, and the power, and the glory, for ever. Amen.

MATTHEW 6:9–13 KJV

They who seek the throne of grace find that throne in every place;
If we live a life of prayer, God is present everywhere.

OLIVER HOLDEN

THE LORD'S PRAYER

ALL IS WELL

A living, loving God can and does make His presence felt, can and does speak to us in the silence of our hearts, can and does warm and caress us till we no longer doubt that He is near, that He is here.

BRENNAN MANNING

If God is present at every point in space, if we cannot go where He is not, cannot even conceive of a place where He is not, why then has not that Presence become the one unanswerably celebrated fact of the world? People do not know if God is here. What a difference it would make if they knew.

A. W. TOZER

Before me, even as behind,
God is, and all is well.

JOHN GREENLEAF WHITTIER

From everlasting to everlasting, thou art God.

PSALM 90:2 KJV

ALL IS WELL

SEEN AND UNSEEN

For the truth about God is known to them instinctively. God has put this knowledge in their hearts. From the time the world was created, people have seen the earth and sky and all that God made. They can clearly see his invisible qualities—his eternal power and divine nature. So they have no excuse whatsoever for not knowing God.

ROMANS 1:19–20 NLT

Am I not present everywhere, whether seen or unseen?

JEREMIAH 23:24 MSG

So we fix our eyes not on what is seen, but on what is unseen. For what is seen is temporary, but what is unseen is eternal.

2 CORINTHIANS 4:18 NIV

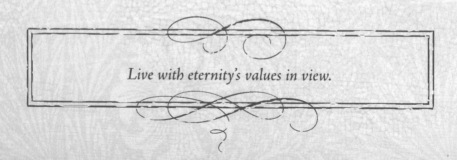

Live with eternity's values in view.

SEEN AND UNSEEN

OVERFLOWING PRAISE

All enjoyment spontaneously overflows into praise.... The world rings with praise...
walkers praising the countryside, players praising their favorite game.... I think
we delight to praise what we enjoy because the praise not merely expresses but
completes the enjoyment; it is the appointed consummation.

C. S. LEWIS

God's pursuit of praise from us and our pursuit of pleasure in Him are one and the
same pursuit. God's quest to be glorified and our quest to be satisfied reach their
goal in this one experience: our delight in God which overflows in praise.

JOHN PIPER

Earth, with her thousand voices, praises God.

SAMUEL TAYLOR COLERIDGE

O sing unto the Lord a new song:
sing unto the Lord, all the earth.

PSALM 96:1 KJV

OVERFLOWING PRAISE

_____

_____

_____

_____

_____

_____

_____

_____

_____

_____

_____

_____

_____

_____

_____

_____

_____

_____

_____

_____

_____

SEEK THE LORD

The God who made the world and everything in it is the Lord of heaven and earth…. He himself gives all men life and breath and everything else…. God did this so that men would seek him and perhaps reach out for him and find him, though he is not far from each one of us. "For in him we live, and move, and have our being."

ACTS 17:24–28 NIV

I love those who love me; and those who diligently seek me will find me.

PROVERBS 8:17 NASB

God is not an elusive dream or a phantom to chase, but a divine person to know. He does not avoid us, but seeks us. When we seek Him, the contact is instantaneous.

NEVA COYLE

SEEK THE LORD

THE SEA REMAINS THE SEA

Dear Lord, today I thought of the words of Vincent van Gogh, "It is true that there is an ebb and flow, but the sea remains the sea." You are the sea. Although I may experience many ups and downs in my emotions and often feel great shifts in my inner life, you remain the same.... There are days of sadness and days of joy; there are feelings of guilt and feelings of gratitude; there are moments of failure and moments of success; but all of them are embraced by your unwavering love.

My only real temptation is to doubt your love...to remove myself from the healing radiance of your love. To do these things is to move into the darkness of despair.

O Lord, sea of love and goodness, let me not fear too much the storms and winds of my daily life, and let me know that there is ebb and flow...but that the sea remains the sea. Amen.

HENRI J. M. NOUWEN

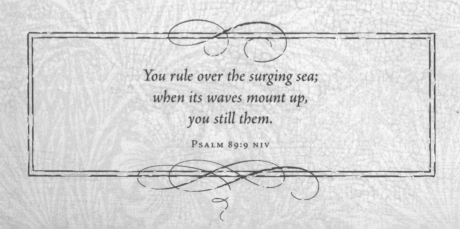

You rule over the surging sea;
when its waves mount up,
you still them.

PSALM 89:9 NIV

_____

_____

_____

_____

_____

_____

_____

_____

_____

_____

_____

_____

_____

_____

_____

_____

To All Generations

Know therefore that the Lord your God is God; he is the faithful God, keeping his covenant of love to a thousand generations of those who love him and keep his commands.

DEUTERONOMY 7:9 NIV

For the Lord is good; his mercy is everlasting; and his truth endureth to all generations.

PSALM 100:5 KJV

Thy kingdom is an everlasting kingdom, and thy dominion endureth throughout all generations.

PSALM 145:13 KJV

I will sing of the mercies of the Lord for ever: with my mouth will I make known thy faithfulness to all generations.

PSALM 89:1 KJV

In following our everlasting God,
we touch the things that last forever.

TO ALL GENERATIONS

_____

_____

_____

_____

_____

_____

_____

_____

_____

_____

_____

_____

_____

_____

_____

_____

_____

_____

_____

_____

_____

_____

_____

GOD LISTENS

Open wide the windows of our spirits and fill us full of light; open wide the door of our hearts, that we may receive and entertain Thee with all our powers of adoration.

CHRISTINA ROSSETTI

We come this morning—

Like empty pitchers to a full fountain,

With no merits of our own,

O Lord—open up a window of heaven…

And listen this morning.

JAMES WELDON JOHNSON

God listens in compassion and love, just like we do when our children come to us.
He delights in our presence.

RICHARD J. FOSTER

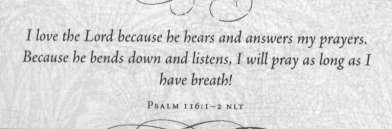

I love the Lord because he hears and answers my prayers.
Because he bends down and listens, I will pray as long as I
have breath!

PSALM 116:1–2 NLT

GOD LISTENS

DELIGHT IN THE LORD

Delight yourself in the Lord and he will give you the desires of your heart. Commit your way to the Lord; trust in him and he will do this: He will make your righteousness shine like the dawn, the justice of your cause like the noonday sun.

PSALM 37:4–6 NIV

Send forth your light and your truth, let them guide me; let them bring me to your holy mountain, to the place where you dwell. Then will I go to the altar of God, to God, my joy and my delight.

PSALM 43:3–4 NIV

*Our fulfillment comes in knowing God's glory,
loving Him for it, and delighting in it.*

DELIGHT IN THE LORD

NEW LIGHT

I cannot open mine eyes,

But Thou art ready there to catch

My morning soul, and sacrifice…

Teach me Thy love to know;

That this new light, which now I see,

May both the work and Workman show:

Then by a sunbeam I will climb to Thee.

GEORGE HERBERT

When we allow God the privilege of shaping our lives, we discover new depths of purpose and meaning. What a joyful thought to realize you are a chosen vessel for God—perfectly suited for His use.

JONI EARECKSON TADA

The Lord God loves you. He says to you, "Behold, I make all things new. Yes, even you!"

BASILEA SCHLINK

Lord, you are our Father. We are the clay, and you are the potter. We are all formed by your hand.

ISAIAH 64:8 NLT

N E W   L I G H T

BOUNDLESS STRENGTH

I ask the God of our Master, Jesus Christ, the God of glory—to make you intelligent and discerning in knowing him personally, your eyes focused and clear, so that you can see exactly what it is he is calling you to do, grasp the immensity of this glorious way of life he has for Christians, oh, the utter extravagance of his work in us who trust him—endless energy, boundless strength!

EPHESIANS 1:17–19 MSG

The Lord is great, and greatly to be praised…. The Lord made the heavens. Honour and majesty are before him: strength and beauty are in his sanctuary…. Give unto the Lord glory and strength. Give unto the Lord the glory due unto his name.

PSALM 96:4–8 KJV

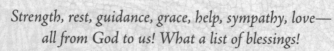

Strength, rest, guidance, grace, help, sympathy, love—
all from God to us! What a list of blessings!

EVELYN STENBOCK

BOUNDLESS STRENGTH

TOTALLY AWARE

God is every moment totally aware of each one of us. Totally aware in intense concentration and love.... No one passes through any area of life, happy or tragic, without the attention of God with him.

EUGENIA PRICE

Because God is responsible for our welfare, we are told to cast all our care upon Him, for He cares for us. God says, "I'll take the burden—don't give it a thought—leave it to Me." God is keenly aware that we are dependent upon Him for life's necessities.

BILLY GRAHAM

You are God's created beauty and the focus of His affection and delight.

JANET L. WEAVER SMITH

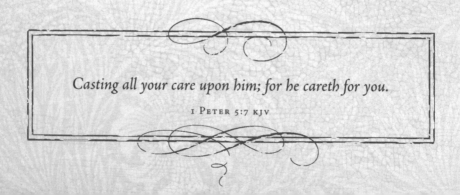

Casting all your care upon him; for he careth for you.

1 PETER 5:7 KJV

TOTALLY AWARE

THE LOVE OF GOD

Who shall separate us from the love of Christ? Shall trouble or hardship or persecution or famine or nakedness or danger or sword? No, in all these things we are more than conquerors through him who loved us. For I am convinced that neither death nor life, neither angels nor demons, neither the present nor the future, nor any powers, neither height nor depth, nor anything else in all creation, will be able to separate us from the love of God that is in Christ Jesus our Lord.

ROMANS 8:35–39 NIV

Nothing can separate you from His love, absolutely nothing.... God is enough for time, and God is enough for eternity. God is enough!

HANNAH WHITALL SMITH

THE LOVE OF GOD

_____

_____

_____

_____

_____

_____

_____

_____

_____

_____

_____

_____

_____

_____

_____

_____

_____

_____

_____

_____

_____

_____

WHAT MATTERS

The God who created, names, and numbers the stars in the heavens also numbers the hairs of my head…. He pays attention to very big things and to very small ones. What matters to me matters to Him, and that changes my life.

ELISABETH ELLIOT

What matters supremely is not the fact that I know God, but the larger fact which underlies it—the fact that He knows me. I am graven on the palms of His hands. I am never out of His mind. All my knowledge of Him depends on His sustained initiative in knowing me. I know Him because He first knew me, and continues to know me.

J. I. PACKER

One hundred years from today your present income will be inconsequential. One hundred years from now it won't matter if you got that big break…. It will greatly matter that you knew God.

DAVID SHIBLEY

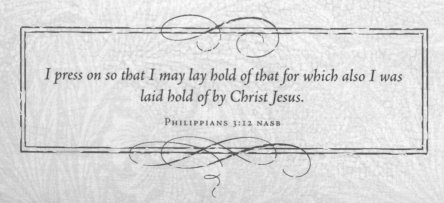

I press on so that I may lay hold of that for which also I was laid hold of by Christ Jesus.

PHILIPPIANS 3:12 NASB

WHAT MATTERS

ROADS TO TRAVEL

If you want to live well, make sure you understand all of this. If you know what's good for you, you'll learn this inside and out. God's paths get you where you want to go. Right-living people walk them easily; wrong-living people are always tripping and stumbling.

HOSEA 14:9 MSG

Enter through the narrow gate. For wide is the gate and broad is the road that leads to destruction, and many enter through it. But small is the gate and narrow the road that leads to life, and only a few find it.

MATTHEW 7:13 NIV

And how blessed all those in whom you live, whose lives become roads you travel; they wind through lonesome valleys, come upon brooks, discover cool springs and pools brimming with rain! God-traveled, these roads curve up the mountain, and at the last turn—Zion! God in full view!

PSALM 84:5–7 MSG

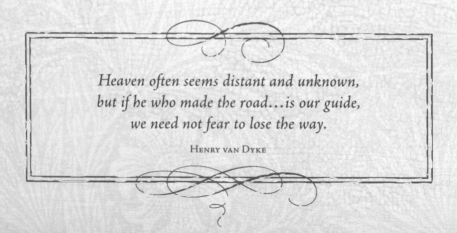

Heaven often seems distant and unknown,
but if he who made the road…is our guide,
we need not fear to lose the way.

HENRY VAN DYKE

ROADS TO TRAVEL

HIS BEAUTIFUL WORLD

The God who holds the whole world in His hands wraps himself in the splendor of the sun's light and walks among the clouds.

Forbid that I should walk through Thy beautiful world with unseeing eyes:
Forbid that the lure of the market-place should ever entirely steal my heart away from the love of the open acres and the green trees:
Forbid that under the low roof of workshop or office or study I should ever forget Thy great overarching sky.

JOHN BAILLIE

Our Creator would never have made such lovely days, and given us the deep hearts to enjoy them, above and beyond all thought, unless we were meant to be immortal.

NATHANIEL HAWTHORNE

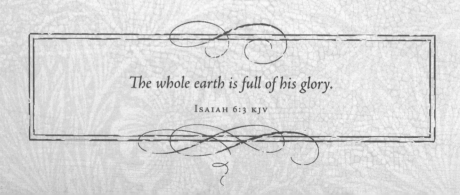

The whole earth is full of his glory.

ISAIAH 6:3 KJV

H I S B E A U T I F U L W O R L D

A WAY OUT

But remember that the temptations that come into your life are no different from what others experience. And God is faithful. He will keep the temptation from becoming so strong that you can't stand up against it. When you are tempted, he will show you a way out so that you will not give in to it.

1 CORINTHIANS 10:13 NLT

For troubles without number surround me; my sins have overtaken me, and I cannot see. They are more than the hairs of my head, and my heart fails within me. Be pleased, O Lord, to save me; O Lord, come quickly to help me.

PSALM 40:12–13 NIV

I need Thy presence every passing hour; what but Thy grace can foil the tempter's power? Who like Thyself my guide and stay can be? Through cloud and sunshine, O abide with me.

HENRY FRANCIS LYTE

A WAY OUT

INFINITE LOVE

An infinite God can give all of himself to each of His children. He does not distribute himself that each may have a part, but to each one He gives all of himself as fully as if there were no others…. His love has not changed. It hasn't cooled off, and it needs no increase because He has already loved us with infinite love and there is no way that infinitude can be increased…. He is the same yesterday, today, and forever!

A. W. TOZER

Infinite and yet personal, personal and yet infinite, God may be trusted because He is the True One. He is true, He acts truly, and He speaks truly…. God's truthfulness is therefore foundational for His trustworthiness.

OS GUINNESS

At the very heart and foundation of all God's dealings with us, however dark and mysterious they may be, we must dare to believe in and assert the infinite, unmerited, and unchanging love of God.

L. B. COWMAN

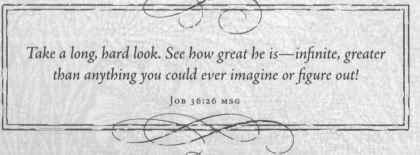

Take a long, hard look. See how great he is—infinite, greater than anything you could ever imagine or figure out!

JOB 36:26 MSG

INFINITE LOVE

From Sea to Sea

The earth is the Lord's, and the fulness thereof; the world, and they that dwell therein. For he hath founded it upon the seas, and established it upon the floods.

Psalm 24:1–2 KJV

The voice of the Lord is over the waters; the God of glory thunders, the Lord thunders over the mighty waters. The voice of the Lord is powerful; the voice of the Lord is majestic.

Psalm 29:3–4 NIV

The Lord is the great God, the great King above all gods. In his hand are the depths of the earth, and the mountain peaks belong to him. The sea is his, for he made it, and his hands formed the dry land.

Psalm 95:3–5 NIV

He will rule from sea to sea.

Psalm 72:8 NIV

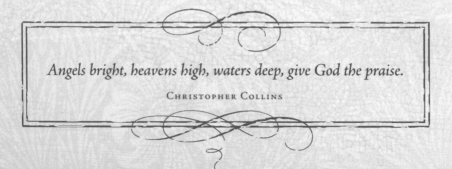

Angels bright, heavens high, waters deep, give God the praise.

Christopher Collins

FROM SEA TO SEA

BY LOVE ALONE

By love alone is God enjoyed; by love alone delighted in, by love alone approached and admired. His nature requires love.

THOMAS TRAHERNE

Love does not allow lovers
to belong anymore to themselves,
but they belong only to the Beloved.

DIONYSIUS

There is an essential connection between experiencing God, loving God, and trusting God. You will trust God only as much as you love Him, and you will love Him to the extent you have touched Him, rather than He has touched you.

BRENNAN MANNING

Love the Lord your God with all your heart, all your soul, and all your strength.

DEUTERONOMY 6:5 NLT

BY LOVE ALONE

PRAISE AND WORSHIP

Praise ye the Lord. Praise God in his sanctuary: praise him in the firmament of his power. Praise him for his mighty acts: praise him according to his excellent greatness. Praise him with the sound of the trumpet: praise him with the psaltery and harp. Praise him with the timbrel and dance: praise him with stringed instruments and organs. Praise him upon the loud cymbals: praise him upon the high sounding cymbals. Let every thing that hath breath praise the Lord. Praise ye the Lord.

PSALM 150:1–6 KJV

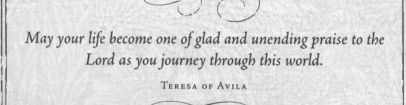

May your life become one of glad and unending praise to the Lord as you journey through this world.

TERESA OF AVILA

PRAISE AND WORSHIP

Every Need

God wants nothing from us except our needs, and these furnish Him with room to display His bounty when He supplies them freely.... Not what I have, but what I do not have, is the first point of contact between my soul and God.

Charles H. Spurgeon

Jesus Christ has brought every need, every joy, every gratitude, every hope of ours before God. He accompanies us and brings us into the presence of God.

Dietrich Bonhoeffer

The "air" which our souls need also envelops all of us at all times and on all sides. God is round about us...on every hand, with many-sided and all-sufficient grace.

Ole Hallesby

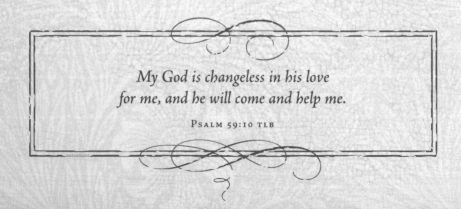

My God is changeless in his love for me, and he will come and help me.

Psalm 59:10 TLB

EVERY NEED

_____

_____

_____

_____

_____

_____

_____

_____

_____

_____

_____

_____

_____

_____

_____

_____

_____

_____

_____

_____

Great Is the Lord

I will exalt you, my God the King; I will praise your name for ever and ever. Every day I will praise you and extol your name for ever and ever. Great is the Lord and most worthy of praise; his greatness no one can fathom. One generation will commend your works to another; they will tell of your mighty acts. They will speak of the glorious splendor of your majesty, and I will meditate on your wonderful works. They will tell of the power of your awesome works, and I will proclaim your great deeds. They will celebrate your abundant goodness and joyfully sing of your righteousness.

Psalm 145:1–7 niv

Worship is transcendent wonder.

Thomas Carlyle

GREAT IS THE LORD

_____

_____

_____

_____

_____

_____

_____

_____

_____

_____

_____

_____

_____

_____

_____

_____

_____

_____

_____

LOVE ONE ANOTHER

You who have received so much love share it with others. Love others the way that God has loved you, with tenderness.

MOTHER TERESA

Let Jesus be in your heart,

Eternity in your spirit,

The world under your feet,

The will of God in your actions.

And let the love of God shine forth from you.

CATHERINE OF GENOA

Every single act of love bears the imprint of God.

Dear friends, since God so loved us, we also ought to love one another.... If we love one another, God lives in us and his love is made complete in us.

I JOHN 4:11–12 NIV

LOVE ONE ANOTHER

THINK ON THESE THINGS

Whatsoever things are true, whatsoever things are honest, whatsoever things are just, whatsoever things are pure, whatsoever things are lovely, whatsoever things are of good report; if there be any virtue, and if there be any praise, think on these things.

PHILIPPIANS 4:8 KJV

The Lord is in his holy Temple; the Lord still rules from heaven. He watches everything closely, examining everyone on earth…. For the Lord is righteous, and he loves justice. Those who do what is right will see his face.

PSALM 11:4, 7 NLT

The fountain of beauty is the heart, and every generous thought illustrates the walls of your chamber.

FRANCIS QUARLES

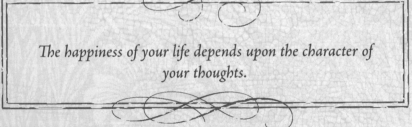

The happiness of your life depends upon the character of your thoughts.

THINK ON THESE THINGS

_____

_____

_____

_____

_____

_____

_____

_____

_____

_____

_____

_____

_____

_____

_____

_____

_____

_____

_____

_____

GOD IS PASSING BY

Friendships, family ties, the companionship of little children, an autumn forest flung in prodigality against a deep blue sky, the intricate design and haunting fragrance of a flower, the counterpoint of a Bach fugue or the melodic line of a Beethoven sonata, the fluted note of bird song, the glowing glory of a sunset: the world is aflame with things of eternal moment.

E. MARGARET CLARKSON

Sunset

The day is done,

The sun has set,

Yet light still tints the sky;

My heart stands still

In reverence,

For God is passing by.

RUTH ALLA WAGER

*Where morning dawns and evening
fades you call forth songs of joy.*

PSALM 65:8 NIV

GOD IS PASSING BY

ACCESSIBLE

Never lose an opportunity of seeing anything that is beautiful; for beauty is God's handwriting—a wayside sacrament. Welcome it in every fair face, in every fair sky, in every fair flower, and thank God for it.

RALPH WALDO EMERSON

The wonder of our Lord is that He is so accessible to us in the common things of our lives: the cup of water…breaking of the bread…welcoming children into our arms…fellowship over a meal…giving thanks. A simple attitude of caring, listening, and lovingly telling the truth.

NANCIE CARMICHAEL

If God is here for us and not elsewhere, then in fact *this place* is holy and *this moment* is sacred.

ISABEL ANDERS

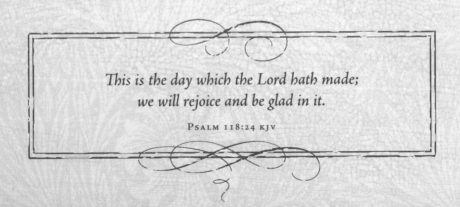

*This is the day which the Lord hath made;
we will rejoice and be glad in it.*

PSALM 118:24 KJV

ACCESSIBLE

> *We need time to dream, time to remember,*
> *and time to reach the infinite. Time to be.*
>
> GLADYS TABER